THE HIGHLY SENSITIVE

How to Stop Emotional Overload, Relieve Anxiety, and Eliminate Negative Energy

JUDY DYER

THE HIGHLY SENSITIVE: How to Stop Emotional Overload,
Relieve Anxiety, and Eliminate Negative Energy
by Judy Dyer

© Copyright 2018 by Judy Dyer

Disclaimer: This book is designed to provide accurate and
authoritative information in regard to the subject matter covered. By
its sale, neither the publisher nor the author is engaged in rendering
psychological or other professional services. If expert assistance or
counseling is needed, the services of a competent professional should
be sought.

ISBN-10: 1720622493
ISBN:13: 978-1720622499

In loving memory of my father,
Thomas Dyer

CONTENTS

CONTENTS

INTRODUCTION

Welcome! Thank you for downloading this guide to overcoming the most common problems faced by Highly Sensitive Persons, or HSPs. You might be a little confused by the term "highly sensitive." In some places, being called "sensitive" is an insult, and you may be wondering whether it's a curse to be born an HSP. There's no denying that HSPs do face some big challenges—they are so much more sensitive than the world around them, after all! But, with the right guidance, you can make peace with your gift.

If you have always wondered why you seem somewhat different from those around you, learning about high sensitivity can come as a big relief. You aren't a freak, and you aren't deficient in any way. In fact, as you read through this book and learn more about HSPs, you'll come to realize how lucky you are to have been born with this gift! There are many people who would love to possess your empathy, appreciation of the fine arts, and capacity to ponder life's big questions.

It's well worth taking the time to understand your sensitive nature. Only then will you be able to lead a lifestyle that perfectly suits your needs. This book will help you take your first steps in coming to terms with your special trait.

In order to maximize the value you receive from this book, I highly encourage you to join our tight-knit community on Facebook. Here you will be able to connect and share with other like-minded HSPs to continue your growth.

Taking this journey alone is not recommended and this can be an excellent support network for you.

It would be great to connect with you there,

Judy Dyer

To Join, Visit: www.pristinepublish.com/empathgroup

YOUR FREE GIFT

Are you weighed down by resentment, anger, or even a desire for revenge against people who have upset you?

If you want to make positive changes to your life and improve your relationships but are held back by past hurts and grievances, download my FREE Guide To Forgiveness For HSPs. It contains a straightforward, step-by-step guide to forgiveness that will help you release negative energy and resentment.

Visit http://pristinepublish.com/forgive

DO YOU ENJOY LISTENING?

If you are someone who prefers to learn by listening or would enjoy a narration as you read along, be sure to check out my HSP Audiobook. It can be listened to for FREE if you're a first time Audible user as part of their free 30-day trial.

Visit: pristinepublish.com/audiobooks

CHAPTER 1

What is an HSP, Anyway?

Have you always been told that you are too sensitive for your own good, that you need to "toughen up," or that you cry too easily? If you're a deep thinker who often feels as though you don't quite fit in, there's a good chance you might be an HSP.

This kind of sensitivity is more common than you might think. Dr. Elaine Aron, famous for her research with HSPs, states that approximately 20% of the population is highly sensitive.

SIGNS OF THE HIGHLY SENSITIVE PERSON – A HELPFUL LIST

How many of the following describe you?

1. A tendency to feel particularly overwhelmed in noisy environments.

2. A preference for smaller gatherings of people rather than large crowds.

3. A good track record of picking up on other people's moods and motives.

4. An ability to notice little changes in the environment.

5. A tendency to be easily moved by music, books, films, and other media.

6. Heightened sensitivity to hunger, pain, medication, and caffeine.

7. A need to recharge and relax alone on a regular basis.

8. An appreciation of good manners and politeness.

9. Difficulty in refusing others' requests for fear of hurting their feelings.

10. Difficulty in forgiving yourself for even the smallest mistakes.

11. Perfectionism and imposter syndrome.

12. Trouble handling conflict and criticism.

You don't have to answer "Yes!" to every item on this list to qualify as an HSP. Trust your intuition. If this list resonates with you, there's a good chance that you have a highly sensitive personality.

D.O.E.S. – A USEFUL WAY TO THINK ABOUT HIGH SENSITIVITY

The D.O.E.S. model is a helpful acronym that explains the HSP profile.

Depth of processing: HSPs have brains that work a little differently from the norm. They process incoming information—sights, sounds, smells, and so on—in a more thorough way. An HSPs mirror neurons—the cells in the brain that help us empathize with others—are more active than average. This explains why HSPs are especially sensitive to other people's moods and feelings and why they are readily overwhelmed in noisy places.

Overstimulation: Overstimulation is inevitable when you have a particularly sensitive brain! An HSP takes longer than the average person to process stimuli, so they soon become overwhelmed and drained in busy or crowded environments. This also accounts for their heightened sensitivity to pain and hunger.

Emotional reactivity: Emotional reactivity is probably what gets HSPs into trouble most often. As they are always "tuned in" to their environment, they cannot help but react strongly to both positive and negative situations. Unfortunately, their negative emotions can become all-consuming if not properly managed. Being so empathetic, they are also prone to picking up on other people's bad moods.

Sensing the subtle: HSPs do not have superhuman powers—they see and hear just about as well as anyone else. However, they do have a special ability to pick up on tiny details in the environment that other people usually miss. For example, if you are an HSP, you may find that you are the first to notice when a vase of flowers has been moved to a different place in a room.

This attention to detail also applies in social settings. An HSP can easily identify deception and ulterior motives in a friend or partner. Even when someone tries to conceal their true nature, an HSP will usually be able to see through the act!

High sensitivity isn't a disorder or an illness. It's just a natural variation that occurs in a minority of the human population. An HSP is born possessing this trait, which cannot be learned or unlearned. Men are just as likely to be highly sensitive as women, so don't assume that you can't be an HSP if you are a man.

HSP MYTHS

High sensitivity isn't well understood. Here are just a few of the most common myths debunked.

HSPs are empaths. All empaths are HSPs, but not all

HSPs are empaths. You can think of an empath as an individual who meets all the criteria for high sensitivity yet has an additional set of abilities. An empath literally feels other people's emotions, whereas HSPs merely sense them. Empaths are also more vulnerable to negative energy and are more likely to report meaningful spiritual and intuitive experiences.

HSPs are all introverts. Whilst the majority of HSPs are introverts, almost one-third (30%) are actually extroverts! Don't dismiss the possibility that you are an HSP just because spending time with other people leaves you feeling energized rather than drained. In fact, HSPs can develop a wide circle of friends because they are so empathetic and intellectually stimulating.

HSPs are just shy. HSPs often like to take their time when processing social situations, especially if they are in a noisy environment. To an outsider, their measured approach might suggest that they are shy. This isn't the case. It's more likely that a quiet HSP is just taking a moment or two to reflect on what is happening around them. They might appear slower to speak than others, but this is because they believe in the power of words and therefore prefer to think about what they want to say before opening their mouths.

HSPs all have anxiety disorders and/or depression. This simply isn't true. High sensitivity describes a way of thinking and relating to the world, whereas anxiety disorders and depression are mental illnesses. However, it is true that HSPs can become anxious and depressed if they don't understand their own needs. They can also experience great suffering if those around them cannot, or will not, understand them. Later in this book, you'll learn how to keep yourself healthy and happy.

HSPs all have Autism Spectrum Disorders (ASD). People with ASD sometimes have problems processing sensory information, and they can become overloaded as a result. In some cases, those with ASD can experience "meltdowns" triggered by excessive sensory input. It's easy to see why people conflate "highly sensitive" and "autistic."

However, there is a fundamental difference between being an HSP and having an ASD. An ASD is a developmental disorder, not a trait or personality type. To be diagnosed with ASD, an individual must show "persistent deficits in social communication and social interaction across multiple contexts." HSPs do not have problems communicating with other people, and the majority are skilled at social interaction.

HSPs have Attention Deficit Hyperactivity Disorder (ADHD), or Attention Deficit Disorder (ADD), and that's why they are so reactive to stimuli. This is simply untrue. ADHD and ADD are psychiatric disorders that usually require treatment, whereas high sensitivity is a natural variation that occurs in one-fifth of the population.

This confusion arises because there are some points of

similarity between HSPs and those with ADHD/ADD. Both groups tend to be perfectionists, they both have a well-developed sense of intuition, they both enjoy daydreaming, and they both like to help other people. They also share an appreciation for the arts, frequently feel the need to express themselves creatively, and believe in standing up for the oppressed. As an HSP, you may find that you naturally gravitate towards people with ADD or ADHD.

However, there are a few signs that separate an HSP from someone with ADHD. For the most part, HSPs have the ability to concentrate for prolonged periods of time, which is usually a difficult task for those with ADHD. HSPs are usually better at following the thread of a conversation. However, an overstimulated HSP soon feels overwhelmed, and they might find it hard to complete a task.

To complicate matters further, it's possible to be highly sensitive and be diagnosed with ADHD or ADD at the same time! However, as a general rule, you are likely to be one or the other. Reading this book will help you gain clarity on this point. If you are still unsure, consider consulting a medical professional to gain a definitive diagnosis.

HSPs are rare. Twenty percent of the population are HSPs. You could argue that this makes them relatively unusual, but it's hardly a "rare" trait. To put it into perspective, at least one child in every classroom is an HSP, and there might be a few dozen working in a large company! Assuming you know at least five people besides yourself, there's a good chance you know another HSP.

HSPs are more gifted, intelligent, or creative than the average person. This may or may not be true—we don't have enough information yet to know either way! Dr. Elaine Aron, highly-regarded sensitivity expert, takes the view that HSPs and non-HSPs are probably equally as intelligent and creative.

It's obvious when someone is highly sensitive. If you are an HSP, you have probably chosen to hide your trait from time to time. Most highly sensitive people have taught themselves to conceal their true nature for fear of being judged. For example, if your parents made you feel bad just because you happened to have a sensitive nature, it's almost inevitable that you would get into the habit of pretending to be "normal." As an HSP, you have been blessed with a strong sense of intuition, but don't beat yourself up if another HSP slips past you—over time, sensitive people can become highly accomplished at putting up a façade.

HSPs can be "normal" if they want to change. It's true that an HSP can *act* "normal," but this doesn't mean that they can turn their sensitivity on and off at will. They certainly don't choose to be more sensitive than the rest of the world.

All HSPs prefer a quiet, boring life with little stimulation. Most HSPs value the opportunity to retreat from the hustle and bustle of the world to relax and recharge, particularly if they've had to spend a lot of time in a busy environment.

However, this definitely does not mean that they want to stay at home all the time! HSPs tend to be curious about the world around them, so they will happily go out and explore it. Not only that, but extroverted HSPs can thrive in social situations that entail talking to lots of people.

HSPs are weak. Sensitive doesn't mean "weak" or "frail." To survive as an HSP in a world that doesn't understand sensitivity requires strength and determination—in fact, you can't afford to be weak if you're an HSP!

HSPs don't have successful careers. It's true that HSPs have different requirements when it comes to the workplace. For example, as an HSP, you probably dislike jobs that require you to work in chaotic environments for hours at a time. However, as long as you understand and accommodate your own needs, there is no reason you can't enjoy a great career.

The key to having a successful career is noticing your strengths and making the most of them. For instance, as a diplomatic person who is reluctant to hurt anyone's feelings, you are in a great position to put forward constructive criticism and potentially controversial new ideas without causing undue offense. This will gain you respect at work.

There's a lot of information to take in when learning about high sensitivity. Fortunately, you don't have to remember all the finer details. Just bear in mind that, as an HSP, you can't help but process the world in a deeper, arguably more meaningful way than the majority of the population.

Unfortunately, it's hard to manage your feelings if you don't have the tools to do so! Just because you feel emotions intensely doesn't mean you know how to deal with them. In the next chapter, we'll look at how you can develop your emotional intelligence and why these skills can make your life as an HSP much easier.

CHAPTER 2

Dealing with Emotional Overwhelm & Building Your Emotional Intelligence

You're probably familiar with the concept of IQ—a measure of general intelligence—but have you ever thought about your emotional intelligence (EQ)? In order to understand your personality, skills, and needs, it's important that you understand these concepts in detail.

Those with a high IQ are typically good at working with abstract information, spotting patterns, and generally making sense of information. They tend to perform well at school and are thought of as "smart" and "intelligent."

But what does it mean to be emotionally intelligent? In brief, someone with a high EQ is skilled in recognizing and working with their own emotions and those of other people. For example, they are able to identify when they feel sad and then work out what they can do to feel better. A high EQ is also associated with strong relationships and connections to the broader community.

We can break emotional intelligence into three main components.

Emotional awareness: The ability to hone in on how you feel, understand why you are feeling a particular way, and give each feeling a label. Emotionally intelligent people are not afraid of any emotion. They know that feelings are a natural, normal part of the human experience.

Handling emotions: The ability to process your feelings and those of others in a constructive manner. For instance, someone with a high EQ is able to calm themselves down in a high-pressure situation. They are also able to soothe others when they are hurt and cheer them up when necessary.

Harnessing emotions: The ability to channel your emotions in a useful way, for example in solving problems or expressing yourself creatively. For example, an artist who draws on their personal experiences in creating sculptures is demonstrating their emotional intelligence.

Another way of looking at EQ is to think of it as a collection of skills: self-awareness, social awareness, relationship management, and self-management. The stronger your skills in these areas, the higher your EQ.

WHAT DOES ALL THIS HAVE TO DO WITH HSPS?

You may be highly sensitive, but this doesn't mean that you know how to handle your feelings. HSPs are often good at self-awareness and social awareness, but not so good at self and relationship management. This means that they can become emotionally overwhelmed, which can take a toll on their mental and physical health. As an HSP, you will always be susceptible to emotional overwhelm, but developing your EQ can help you maintain healthy emotional equilibrium.

For example, let's say that you are having a busy day at work. As an HSP, you realize that you feel stressed, and you also know that your colleagues feel pressured. Your emotional awareness allows you to pick up on this quickly. Great, but what should you actually do about it?

This is where many HSPs tend to get stuck. They can detect what's going on in themselves and others, but they are clueless when it comes to managing these feelings in a healthy way. An HSP who allows themselves to be carried away on a tide of their own emotions or gets bogged down in other people's feelings will soon become miserable.

The good news is that you can learn to develop your EQ and learn skills to improve your self-management and relationships. In the short term, repressing your emotions might lead to temporary relief but you cannot keep them locked away forever. Unless you learn how to face up to them, they will linger in your body and mind as stress, tension, and illness.

SELF-MANAGEMENT
Here are a few tips to help you learn how to process your feelings when it feels as though they may consume you.

Ground Yourself in the Moment
Over-analyzing your surroundings and emotions is a recipe for emotional overwhelm. Learning a few basic grounding techniques can keep your stress levels from spiraling out of control. For instance, naming five things you can hear, see, smell, and touch can have a grounding effect.

Some people like to carry a small object or charm in a pocket or purse and hold it in their hand whenever they feel overwhelmed. For instance, you could buy a keyring that carries a positive association for you and squeeze it during stressful times. This can work well but take care not to become too reliant on any one object—if it gets lost, you'll become very stressed! One solution is to buy a packet of small stress balls and put them in your coat pocket, desk drawer, and so on. That way, you will always have one close by, and you won't become too attached to a single item.

You cannot just will your emotions away. Human beings cannot help but react to experiences, whether internal or external. If you tell yourself to "just get over it" or "stop thinking about it," you will only feel worse. Remember that you can't control your reactions, but you can choose how to process your feelings.

The next time you are overwhelmed by emotions, try this exercise as recommended by therapist Dr. Andrea Brandt.

1. Breathe slowly and deeply, in through your nose and then out through your mouth.

2. Cross your arms and hold each of your forearms with the opposite hand. Squeeze. This sensation will help you remain grounded in your body rather than getting caught up in your thoughts and feelings.

3. Recite a mantra or quote that you personally find to have a calming effect, such as "This too shall pass." "No feeling is forever."

4. Remind yourself that no feeling is "bad." It's OK to be angry, sad, and stressed. The problem only comes when you can't manage your feelings properly and do or say harmful things to yourself or others.

Focus on the positive sides of change

Do you feel overwhelmed by change? You aren't the only one—both HSPs and non-HSPs can find it tough to accept! The trick is to make a habit of identifying the positives in the situation, rather than allowing yourself to dwell on what could go wrong.

The next time you catch yourself panicking about a change, take two minutes to write down any positives you can think of. For instance, if you have to look for a new job because of the risk of redundancy, remind yourself that a new role might offer you a new intellectual challenge. You may be planning to move and feeling stressed as a result. It might help to write down what you like most about your new home and neighborhood.

Of course, not all change comes with positives. If you have recently lost a loved one or are facing bankruptcy, even the most optimistic of individuals would agree that it's hard to find a silver lining. As a general rule, try to take a balanced view of a situation. Unless you are staring utter disaster in the face, there's usually at least one or two blessings or lessons you can take from your personal challenges.

Experiment with new ways of expressing and harnessing your emotions

Don't allow your emotions to fester. Once you have identified what you are feeling (as an HSP, you are probably good at labeling your emotions), you may need to vent it in some way. Experiment to find what works for you. For instance, some people find journaling therapeutic, while others channel their feelings through sports, art, singing, or even just punching a cushion or pillow really hard! As long as you aren't hurting yourself or someone else, do whatever necessary to make yourself feel better.

Feelings are not, in and of themselves, "bad" or something to be feared. They can be a constructive force for change, especially when you harness them in a healthy manner. If you are going through a particularly turbulent time, think of ways you could use the power generated by your emotions to make a positive change. For example, if you have recently escaped an abusive relationship and feel angry and sad on behalf of others in similar situations, you could consider taking on a volunteer role at a local organization serving victims of domestic violence.

Use The Healing Power Of Crystals

Carrying a grounding crystal (such as rose quartz or black tourmaline) in your pocket can help absorb negative energy and reduce your stress levels. They are also excellent meditation aids – hold your favorite stone as you meditate to enjoy greater relaxation. We'll take a closer look at crystals and their special powers later in the book.

MANAGE STRESS BEFORE IT TAKES HOLD

Emotional overwhelm can occur in response to a specific trigger, but sometimes it seems to have no particular cause. This can be frightening because it feels as though you have no control over your own mind. If you start experiencing emotional overwhelm and don't understand why, take a look at your general stress levels. Background stress can lead to seemingly random emotional outbursts that may come and go without warning.

The solution is to take preventative measures that reduce stress levels and keep your emotions on an even keel. HSPs often respond well to regular meditation practices. You don't need to set aside hours each day—just ten minutes of meditation will offer significant benefits.

To get started with meditation, turn off your phone and any other sources of noise and seat yourself in a comfortable chair or on the floor. Close your eyes and take a few deep breaths. Your goal isn't to empty your mind of all thoughts—doing so is virtually impossible. The purpose of meditation is to help you separate yourself from the mental debris and junk we all have whirling through our heads. It trains you to become a detached observer and teaches you that the majority of thoughts are transient and meaningless.

Focus on your breathing. When your mind drifts, as it inevitably will, do not resist it. Remember, you are acting as an observer. See your thoughts and feelings as clouds or balloons. Let them pass you by. With practice, your thoughts will seem less threatening, which will benefit your everyday life. You'll start to realize that even strong emotions do not last forever.

RELATIONSHIP MANAGEMENT

HSPs often love to form meaningful connections with others, and they typically have a good idea of what those around them are thinking. However, this doesn't necessarily mean that your relationships will run smoothly! From time to time, your sensitive nature can make things challenging.

Try not to take criticism personally

Most HSPs are perfectionists and struggle to take criticism.

This presents a dilemma! On one hand, you want to learn from your mistakes and know that you can benefit from other people's advice. You know that receiving criticism can be helpful. At the same time, you can't help but feel personally attacked when someone suggests that you should be doing something different.

The simplest yet most effective way to deal with criticism is to separate yourself from your work. When someone gives you feedback, remember they are referring to your work, not you as a person. For example, if your boss tells you that you need to rewrite a section of a report, this doesn't mean that you are a failure who can never be trusted to produce good work. Unless you have good reason to suspect otherwise, assume the other person is evaluating only what you have *done*, not who you *are*.

It may seem scary, but receiving feedback and constructive criticism gets easier with practice. Actively seeking out criticism is probably the last thing you want to do, but you'll be surprised how soon you can learn to take other people's advice. If you receive negative feedback, turn it into a list of actionable bullet points. This will give you a sense of control.

For example, if your boss tells you that a report you've written is too long-winded and contains too many statistics, simply writing "Cut sentence length, take out at least a third of the numbers, and use less jargon" gives you a starting point when making revisions.

Another useful tip is to record any positive feedback you receive. You might have noticed that you have the habit of remembering only the negative things people say. Perhaps you discount compliments altogether and worry that your ego will get too big if you believe the nice things your family and friends tell you. Rest assured that this isn't the case. If someone gives you praise, trust that it's for a good reason.

Learn how to handle conflict in a constructive way

Are you conflict-averse? Many HSPs hate the thought of arguing with someone else. Conflict makes the average HSP feel overwhelmed, and the aftereffects can last for days. Fortunately, reframing conflict and learning a few tricks that nurture your relationships can help you navigate it with grace.

For a start, remember that when someone is angry with you, they are angry because their perceptions have led them to feel a certain way, and their image of you isn't necessarily accurate. Keep this in mind and conflict will start to feel less personal. You can never control someone else's perceptions, but you do have the power to choose what *you* do and say.

The key to handling any argument is to first understand how the other person developed their opinion or arrived at a particular conclusion, then gently explain why you believe (or know) that this perspective is incorrect. This requires a lot of diplomacy, but luckily for you, HSPs tend to be naturally skilled in this area! Don't attempt to impose your opinion or will at any cost. Tell yourself that you'll get the best results when you try to really understand someone else's point of view instead of trying to "win."

Remind yourself that conflict may be unpleasant, but

it will help you develop strong communication skills that will serve you well in the future. For instance, having an argument with your partner is no fun, but it may help you at a later date when you need to stand up to a controlling boss. Handling conflicts can also boost your self-esteem—a reminder that you are capable of leaving your comfort zone.

Conflict with those closest to you can be painful, but sometimes it is necessary if the relationship is to move forward. For instance, if your best friend tells you some unpleasant home truths about your friendship during an argument, this may hurt; but it gives the two of you an opportunity to clear the air. Remember that if someone raises their worries directly, it means they probably care a great deal about your relationship.

Finally, you can always ask for some time out from an argument. There is no law that says everyone must resolve their differences in a single conversation! If you need a few minutes to compose yourself or to come to terms with everything that has been said, excuse yourself for a little while. However, don't just leave the room with no explanation, as this will appear dismissive and aggressive.

Draw up firm boundaries

Everyone, highly sensitive or not, needs to draw up and maintain healthy boundaries in their relationships. Boundaries let other people know what you will and will not accept from them. For example, in a healthy relationship, both people have boundaries they erect to keep them safe from abuse. Specifically, they will both make it clear that they will not tolerate any form of mistreatment, and anyone who breaks this rule will face consequences.

Whatever your boundaries may be, you need to enforce them. For instance, you might have set a boundary regarding text messages and the time of day at which you will and won't reply. Your rule might be, "I don't read or respond to messages after dinner, which is around 8 p.m." In deciding this rule, you are setting a boundary—others cannot expect you to read or reply to their messages late in the evening. This kind of boundary keeps you from getting too involved in other people's drama or problems, thereby safeguarding your own emotional wellbeing.

Even if you are clear about your boundaries, there will still be those who might try to violate them. To continue with the above example, one or two of your friends might still expect a reply and be offended when you stick to your boundaries. The good news is that if you are consistent and assertive (whilst remaining polite), others will usually come to respect you for standing up for your own needs.

In order to set firm, healthy boundaries, you need to learn how to say "no." In the next chapter, you'll discover how to do precisely that.

CHAPTER 3

How to Say "No" Without Hurting Others

n the previous chapter, we talked about the relationship management skills you need to develop to be a happy HSP. One of these skills is so important that it deserves a chapter of its own.

As an HSP, you might have noticed that it's hard for you to say "no" to other people. HSPs tend to value good manners, and they don't like the thought of hurting anyone's feelings. There's nothing wrong with wanting to help out or show some consideration, but always saying "yes," even when you really want to yell "no!" comes at a cost.

Over time, you'll begin to resent those who ask you for favors. You might even turn into a martyr, thinking and saying things like, "Why does everyone else expect me to do everything for them?" and "I never have enough time to myself—my whole life is just one errand after another." You might not stop and realize that if you don't learn how to say "no," you are basically allowing other people to use you as a servant!

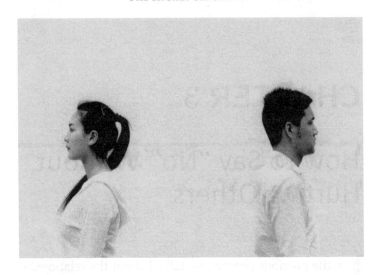

When you agree to take on too many projects or chores, you place yourself at risk of emotional overwhelm. Remember, HSPs often become stressed when confronted by a long to-do list. Don't fight against your nature just for the sake of helping someone else. This is particularly true if the other person in question doesn't often go out of their way to lend you a hand. Relationships don't have to be a perfect 50/50 split, but there's no need to wear yourself out helping someone who takes you for granted.

Given that HSPs are likely to be perfectionists, it's perhaps unsurprising that they are usually among the most competent individuals in a workplace. This has obvious advantages—your chances of success increase if you know what you're doing—but there's one notable downside. When everyone knows that you are a capable person who doesn't like to hurt anyone's feelings, they will start to ask you to take on more work. Perhaps you've even had the experience of being assigned leadership or management duties despite the fact you'd rather chew off your own arm than lead a team. "No" is a two-letter word with the power to save your sanity.

Contrary to what you might believe, saying "no" doesn't make you a bad or selfish person. We all need and deserve to have our own feelings taken into account when making decisions. Here are a few simple but effective ways you can say "no" and keep your relationships intact.

Make "no" the first word that comes out of your mouth. Assertive people start with a firm "no" when declining a request. Ideally, you'll be able to give a short, simple answer that leaves the other person with no doubt as to where you stand.

For example:

"No, thank you, I can't."

"No, I don't have time today."

"No, that won't be possible."

"No, there isn't space in my schedule for that."

If someone continues to push you, they are in the wrong—not you.

Just because saying "no" feels unpleasant, doesn't mean that it isn't the right response. For example, suppose someone asks you on a date. If you happen to be in a relationship, simply saying, "No, thank you, I'm not single," will work fine. But what if you just don't find the other person attractive and don't want to hurt their feelings? You could lie and say that you're already seeing someone, which might be a good idea if the person asking you is a stranger. However, if the two of you move in the same social circles, it won't be too long before they realize that you are, in fact, single.

In this situation, you need to remind yourself that saying "no" is the only humane option. The alternative is to do something that will make both of you unhappy further down the line. In the case of declining a date, it's far better to endure a few moments of awkwardness than to date someone for several weeks (or even months) before working up the courage to tell them that you were not interested in the first place.

Remember too that a reasonable person will be able to tolerate a "no thanks." Your only obligation is to remain civil, thank them for asking, and decline with grace. If they continue to ask despite your refusal or start to harass you, they are the one with a problem!

Do not apologize. Apologies are only appropriate when you have done something wrong. Politely turning down a request isn't morally wrong or even rude, so there's no reason to say sorry. If the asker continues to put you under pressure, they are the one who should be apologizing, not you. Instead of saying "sorry," you can soften a refusal with phrases like "No, thank you. I would like to but ...," "No, that won't be possible because ...," and "No, thank you. It's a shame, but I can't do it because ..."

Keep your body language positive. When saying "no," make a conscious effort to relax your shoulders, make eye contact with the other person, and smile politely. You don't have to be aggressive, just assertive. It may sound silly, but it can help to practice declining a request in front of the mirror!

Do not make excuses. There's no need to devise an elaborate explanation or excuse for why you cannot do something. Not only is a refusal a complete answer in its own right, but elaborate cover stories can come back to haunt you. Even if you pride yourself on having an excellent memory, there's a chance that you'll forget exactly what was said, which could result in no small amount of embarrassment later on.

If the other person doesn't realize you are just making an excuse, they might try to "help" you out, and the conversation may soon move into awkward territory. For instance, if you tell someone that you don't want to see a musical with them on Friday night because you can't get a babysitter, they might respond by telling you that they can give you the number of a great babysitter or suggest that the two of you go out the following week instead. You will then be forced to give another excuse!

Use the broken record technique. Have you ever encountered someone who doesn't seem able to take a hint and keeps repeating the same old question over and over again? There are a couple of reasons this happens. Some people are just plain pushy, persistent, and rude. Others might assume that you'll inevitably say "yes" if they keep asking the same question over and over again, particularly if you've always said "yes" in the past.

Fortunately, the broken record technique is an effective way to shut down these people. To use the broken record technique, simply repeat your answer again in exactly the same tone of voice. Maintain the same facial expression, use the same words, and look them straight in the eye every time you respond. After a few rounds, they will begin to feel silly and self-conscious.

If you know someone who wouldn't mind helping, pass on their name. Under no circumstance should you try to pawn someone off onto a third party just because you aren't brave enough to say "no." However, on some occasions, the best thing to do is recommend that the other person approach someone else who might be able to help. For example, if a colleague asks you for help with a project and you already have far too much work to do, it's fine to recommend that they approach someone else who you know has both the time to offer assistance and would be happy to do so.

Compliment the person who asked you a favor. Some people react badly when they hear "no" because they assume that the other person is rejecting them as an individual, along with their request. If you are dealing with someone like this, it's a good idea to offer them a compliment if possible. For example, "You're such a hard worker, I know you'll make the project a success one way or the other" would be a suitable compliment to give someone when telling them that you won't be helping them with their assignment.

If someone is harassing you, outline the consequences. Unfortunately, some people believe that they are entitled to your help and support whether or not you want to give it to them. Occasionally, you will meet someone who becomes angry or even threatening when you turn down their request. It may be tempting to give in for the sake of preserving the peace, but this won't work out well in the long run—they will assume that they can use intimidation tactics to get their own way.

The best approach is to defend your boundary by informing them of the consequences they will face if they continue to push the issue. For example, you could say, "I have already told you that my answer is 'no.' If you continue to ask me inappropriate questions in the workplace, I will report it to an HR representative."

DOES YOUR SELF-IMAGE HINGE ON SAYING "YES"?

You've probably heard time and time again that you are a "nice" person who can always be relied upon. It's a wonderful reputation to have, but has it come to be a central part of your identity? Take a moment to really think about your answer, even if it makes you feel uncomfortable, because it may go some way in explaining why you are so reluctant to turn people down.

No one is totally exempt from caring about what everyone else thinks of them, including HSPs. If you take pride in being the person who never lets anyone down and always lends a hand, you might be reluctant to say "no" because it means losing a part of your identity. It may help to remind yourself that you don't have to say "yes" at every opportunity to be a good person. Think of the nicest people you know. I bet that some of them (if not all of them) have mastered the art of saying "no."

As an HSP, you probably find a lot of satisfaction in helping others but this doesn't mean you have to extend help at every opportunity. Saying "no, thank you" may not come naturally, but it's a skill you can learn. These little words will not only free up your schedule, allowing you to focus on the people and activities that matter most to you, but it will also help you shore up your boundaries and prevent others from taking advantage of you. As you will learn in the next chapter, an unprepared HSP is vulnerable to exploitative individuals, so it's a good idea to remain on your guard.

CHAPTER 4

How to Avoid Falling in Love too Quickly, Filter Out Unhealthy Partners, and Enjoy a Great Relationship

According to sensitivity experts, HSPs are prone to falling in love in a quick and dramatic fashion, which can be an intoxicating, exhilarating experience. Unfortunately, intense love affairs often crash and burn. This can be painful for anyone, but HSPs are particularly vulnerable to heartbreak. It's important to learn how to guard your heart and take a relationship at a steady pace, even if you are tempted to dive straight in at the deep end!

HSPs are not irrational, but they are often driven by their feelings when they meet someone they find attractive. If you are an HSP, you are in danger of pursuing someone who isn't necessarily right for you just because they make you feel good. Another danger comes from settling. Have you ever felt so lonely and misunderstood that you'd be willing to date (or even marry) the first half-decent person who crossed your path? It's OK—many of us have been there! HSPs love emotional intimacy. Unfortunately, if you are too desperate to find someone, your judgment and intuition might take a back seat.

DON'T ASSUME THAT ONLY ONE PERSON CAN MAKE YOU HAPPY

As an HSP, you can't control your feelings, but you can gently challenge some of the more unrealistic ideas you have about love and romance. Idealism is a charming trait, and it inspires some HSPs to change the world. Unfortunately, an HSP in love can fall into the trap of casting someone in the role of "The One" and come to believe that only one other person can make them content.

It's a romantic idea, but it simply isn't true! If you think about it, most people have several relationships before they settle down with a long-term partner. When you are caught up in a whirlwind of daydreams and hormones, it's easy to lose perspective. Remember the EQ skills you learned earlier in this book? Here's the perfect opportunity to put them into practice! They will help you remain grounded and will also provide you with the tools you need to form a healthy bond.

WATCH OUT FOR PEOPLE WITH SERIOUS PROBLEMS

In theory, you might think that an HSP would be drawn to another sensitive person because they both have similar wants and needs in a relationship. In reality, it's a little more complex than that! If you've been dating for a while, you may have noticed a strange pattern emerging. It's likely that some of the people who find you attractive seem to require hours of love, support, and even re-parenting. If you suspect that others see you as an emotion sponge or even as a counselor, you're probably right.

It's not your fault. As an HSP, your natural empathy makes you highly attractive. That's the good news. The bad news is that some people, whether they have malicious intentions or not, are drawn to you in the hope that you can fix them. Being the helpful person that you are, reluctant to risk hurting anyone's feelings, you've probably found yourself taking on the role of armchair psychologist at some point. If you allow this arrangement to continue, you may never be free. You become too emotionally invested in the other person and can't bear to think of them struggling alone.

So, what should you do? Prevention is better than cure. The most important thing you can do is to realize that other people's problems aren't yours to solve, and they certainly shouldn't form the basis of a romantic relationship. If you are dating someone and discover that they have a serious problem or character flaw, think very carefully before continuing.

Ask yourself this: Do I really want to become entangled with someone who appears to have significant psychological and emotional problems? Do I really want to take on the role of someone's unpaid counselor or aide? Do not confuse "tormented" or "in pain" with "intriguing" or "challenging." Base your choice of partner on whether you share values and interests, not on whether you can play the role of helper!

HOW TO SPOT A TOXIC PERSON

Narcissistic individuals and energy vampires target HSPs. They tend to assume that because HSPs love helping others, they will give them the endless supply of attention and validation they so desperately crave. Don't fall for it. They will treat you well at first, then discard or abuse you when they start taking you for granted. Learn the danger signs that signal a narcissist or energy vampire and avoid dating them at all costs.

Here are the key warnings signs that suggest someone may be a narcissist.

1. They like to talk about themselves all the time. At the start of your relationship, they might ask you a lot of questions, but this isn't because they are actually interested in your life—they simply want to hook you in.

2. They sincerely believe that they are "the best" at everything.

3. They believe they deserve everything life has to offer, even if they don't put in much work.

4. They prefer to hang out with people they perceive as "important" or famous. Status is more important to them than meaningful connections.

5. They often leave you feeling drained, confused, or pessimistic after a day or night together. Even if you haven't had an argument and everything seems OK on the surface, they still manage to bring your mood down.

6. They will happily cast themselves in the role of a victim to get what they want.

Here are a few indicators that someone is an energy vampire. Note that not all energy vampires are narcissists, but all narcissists are energy vampires!

1. They see everything through a lens of negativity.

2. They will happily gossip about other people behind their backs, which means they are probably gossiping about you too.

3. They don't congratulate you when you succeed. They may even belittle your achievements.

4. They talk about themselves all the time and expect you to listen to them for hours.

5. They don't respect your boundaries.

6. They are jealous of others who have the material

possessions or type of relationship they want for themselves.

7. They use passive-aggressive behaviors such as giving you the silent treatment when you don't do as they ask.

If you've been blindsided by someone's good looks and charm, it's not always easy to spot these signs. You may be so keen to see someone for what you want them to be, rather than what they are, that you enter a state of denial. Sometimes, you have to learn these lessons the hard way.

Don't beat yourself up. HSPs and non-HSPs alike sometimes chase people who are toxic or simply not right for them. Just don't let yourself make the same mistake twice. If a close friend suggests that you are involved with someone who isn't right for you, try not to get defensive. Listen to what they have to say, and then decide for yourself whether their concerns are justified.

TRUST YOUR INTUITION

Your intuition is one of your greatest gifts as an HSP. Trust it! Your intuition may not always tell you what you want to hear, but it's there for a reason. For instance, suppose you are dating someone who calls regularly, plans great dates, and compliments you all the time, and yet your inner voice tells you that something isn't quite right.

If your intuition is telling you that something's wrong, it's time to back off a little, slow down, and watch for signs indicating that your partner isn't quite everything they appear.

Sometimes a partner may be acting strangely because they are unsure how to conduct themselves in a relationship, or because they are insecure and afraid of doing something "wrong." It's OK to give them a little while to reveal their true selves. In fact, the wisest people make a point of taking their relationships at a slow pace. If the two of you really are right for one another, then what's the rush anyway?

SHOULD YOU DATE ANOTHER HSP?

On the face of it, finding another HSP may seem to be a good idea. After all, you'll be able to understand one another's struggles and personality type, right? Well, yes—but two HSPs won't automatically make for a happy couple.

The typical HSP-HSP pairing runs into problems because both partners are aware, sometimes to a painful extent, of the other person's moods. Each will pick up on their partner's emotional disturbances, which can be exhausting. Because HSPs tend to be people-pleasers, they might both worry about satisfying their partner in all areas of the relationship—sometimes to an excessive degree. When something goes wrong in the relationship, they both tend to assume the blame, which keeps them locked in misery.

On the other hand, if both HSPs are self-aware and continually working on their own self-development, their relationship can be very fulfilling. As long as both partners are willing to openly express their emotions, talk through troublesome issues, air their grievances in a constructive manner, and take responsibility for their own emotions, they can look forward to many years of happiness. However, it's essential that both parties be sufficiently invested in both the relationship and their personal growth.

MAKE PLANS THAT DON'T REVOLVE AROUND YOUR LOVE LIFE

In Chapter 2, you learned that HSPs are often high in self-awareness but lack skills in self-management. This means that you may be painfully aware that you are in love or have a raging crush on someone but aren't sure what to do about it.

Although it's impossible to stop thinking about the other person when you're in love, continuing to build your own life and future will help you maintain a healthy distance and move on if it turns out they aren't right for you. If you allow yourself to focus on the other person to the detriment of your personal development, you'll have so much energy and emotion invested in the relationship that you'll be reluctant to let go. On the other hand, if you have a full and active life, it will be easier to detach from an unhealthy relationship that isn't going anywhere.

Be sure to keep in touch with your friends. Make it a policy never to look to just one other person for emotional nourishment, because you will be in a vulnerable position if they leave you. To some extent, it's normal to spend less time with your friends in the early days of a romantic relationship, but you should never abandon your friends entirely!

SPEAK UP IN THE EARLY DAYS OF THE RELATIONSHIP

As an HSP, you are tuned in to other people's emotions—sometimes to a painful degree. Your empathetic nature and warm heart draws in people who have problems and need someone to listen. Have you ever been told that you are "so easy to talk to" or "such a good listener"? This is a common experience among HSPs. Although it's great to lend emotional support to others, you can end up taking on the role of an emotional sponge or unpaid therapist unless you learn how to balance your own needs with your desire to support others.

Don't let your natural desire to earn someone's love take priority over your own comfort and needs. Learn how to say "no" and stand your ground! In the early stages of a relationship, you may be all too happy to always put your partner first. Unfortunately, this sets a dangerous precedent. It sends your partner a clear signal—"I'm here to make my own needs secondary to yours, and I'm happy to act as your personal servant!"

This attitude rarely results in a healthy relationship. Your partner will assume that you have low self-esteem, that you don't have a mind of your own, or that you are unusually submissive. There's a risk that any relationship that develops will be based on an unequal power dynamic, whereby one person (your partner) drives the relationship, and the other person (you) plays the role of servant and passenger. You might wake up months or even years later wondering where your life has gone!

Stop Expecting Perfection in Your Relationships

As one of nature's perfectionists, the harsh reality of relationships can seem like too much for you to handle. For example, most couples fight from time to time, and you should expect a degree of conflict between yourself and your partner. In fact, if the two of you never fight, it's likely that one or both of you are repressing your true needs and opinions. This isn't healthy!

If you are serious about finding and keeping a long-term relationship, you must accept that there is no such thing as the perfect partner, and there is no such thing as the perfect relationship. This doesn't mean you have to settle for the first person you find, just that you need to be prepared to compromise in some situations.

You also need to be open to constructive criticism and feedback and be willing to speak up in order to get your needs met. It may not be romantic, but no one—not even HSPs—can read minds! Don't fall back on unrealistic romantic notions such as true love entails knowing precisely what the other person thinks.

Why HSPs Find It particularly Hard to Deal with a Break-Up

It's fair to say that few people feel good when their relationship comes to an end. Even if we have known for a long time that our partner isn't the one for us, it's still painful. Unfortunately, as an HSP, you are even more vulnerable to the difficult feelings that accompany heartbreak. Whereas most people will feel sad and empty for a while following a breakup, HSPs often feel as though their world is literally collapsing around them.

If you are recovering from a broken relationship, remember that it's normal for HSPs to require a longer healing period than the majority of the population. It's harder for you to let go of the feelings and memories associated with your former partner, along with the hopes and dreams you had for the future. This is true even if you were the one who ended it! Imaginative HSPs can spend hours agonizing over what they could or should have done differently, or even picturing what their partner might be doing without them.

What's the best way to deal with a breakup as an HSP? You may have read books or articles advocating that you go "No Contact" with a former partner once the relationship has ended. To put it simply, going No Contact means that you do not see, call, or talk to your ex. Neither should you stalk their social media profile or ask mutual friends how they are doing.

In some cases, it isn't possible to go completely No Contact. However, it's probably the best thing to do if you're an HSP. Why? Because it gives you the best chance of moving on. In the short term, it will feel like agony; but in the long term, you will be much better off. It keeps you from feeding your own obsession and encourages you to look towards the future. No Contact also keeps you from running back into your ex's arms only to be hurt again. Trust that they are an ex for a reason. If the two of you were right for one another, the relationship would not have ended. Remember too that there is more than one person in the world who can make you happy.

The period following a breakup is also the perfect time to practice your self-management skills. Specifically, think of ways you can channel and come to terms with your feelings. Don't just sit on them and hope that they go away! Talk to a trusted friend, seek out a therapist, write about your feelings, take up a new hobby—do whatever it takes, as long as it doesn't hurt your physical or mental health.

Finding the right romantic relationship can be tough for an HSP, but there's no need to feel disheartened. A non-HSP can develop relationship skills and learn from their mistakes, and you can do the same! Relationships can be challenging for everyone, regardless of where they fall on the sensitivity scale. Yes, you might experience the pain of heartbreak more acutely, but you also have the capacity for deep love and affection.

CHAPTER 5

How to Eliminate Negative Energy

A s an HSP, you are much more vulnerable than others to the effects of negative energy, whether it comes from other people or the environment. Everyone reacts differently when exposed to it, but common symptoms include fatigue, feelings of nausea, headaches, muscle aches, and a drop in motivation. Negative energy can make you physically and mentally ill, so it's vital that you learn how to eliminate it! In this chapter, you'll learn several techniques that will protect you from its effects.

WORK ON CULTIVATING A POSITIVE ATTITUDE

There is quite enough negative energy in the world already, so why add to it? The Law of Attraction states that your personal vibration and energy level determines who and what comes into your life. In practice, this means that if you decide to look upon the universe with an open mind and loving heart, you will attract positive people and energy.

In a world full of negative media that encourages us to think about what is going wrong rather than all the positive things that are going on all around us, this is easier said than done. You need to be proactive in changing your attitude. Start by cutting down the amount of time you spend watching and reading the news. Yes, it's good to stay informed when it comes to current affairs, but the majority of news media is full of sensational stories that are produced to "entertain" rather than inform.

Choose to be optimistic. Some of us are naturally more inclined to see the sunny side of any situation, but anyone can learn to be more positive. Watch your own thoughts. What do you think when you open your eyes in the morning? Do you look forward to the day ahead, or do you just want to roll over and go back to sleep?

Every morning, make a point of asking yourself what you are looking forward to in the coming hours. Just before you go to sleep each night, give thanks for at least ten things you enjoyed that day. They can be big things, but the little things count too. For example, be sure to give thanks to the universe if you enjoyed a fantastic cup of coffee with your breakfast or found a free parking space the moment you arrived at the mall that afternoon.

Try keeping a positivity journal. Every day, write down a few things for which you are grateful, together with any quotes that inspire you or compliments you have received from others. You can also record your hopes and dreams for the future. If you are working towards a particular goal, you can monitor your progress.

HARNESS THE POWER OF EARTH, WATER, OR FIRE

Earth, water, and fire can all be used to absorb and transform negative energy. Begin by meditating for a few minutes and clarifying your intentions—to discharge the negative energy that has been building within you. Imagine it moving as a single, dark mass down your arms and into your hands. To discharge it, place your hands in water (ideally, free-flowing water found in a natural environment, but a shower will also work), directly onto the ground outside, or towards a naked flame.

As you do so, picture the negative energy flowing out of your body, through your palms and into the element. Don't worry about spreading negative energy—each element has an infinite capacity to reshape it and deliver it back to the universe as a positive force.

BRING NATURE INDOORS

You've probably noticed that it's easier to feel positive when spending time outside. Trees, grass, flowers, and running water all filter negative energy and promote a sense of well-being. However, it isn't always possible to simply take a walk when you're stressed or upset.

Luckily, you can bring nature indoors! Start by placing at least one plant in each room. This will foster a positive atmosphere that will make it easier to shake off negative energy. Some varieties are particularly beneficial.

Bamboo

A favorite of Feng Shui practitioners, bamboo is considered a potent symbol of luck and health. It represents the wood element, which improves general vitality and promotes positive energy. Traditionally, a bamboo display is made up of an odd number of stalks, as this is thought to bring more luck. Keep it in a bowl of shallow water out of direct sunlight.

Sage

Sage is popular for its ability to remove negative energy from the environment. As a bonus, it also has a pleasant smell, making it a good choice for kitchens and conservatories. Sage plants are prone to drying out so ensure that their soil is kept moist.

Peace Lilies

A peace lily purifies the air around it, removing harmful gases and toxins such as carbon monoxide and benzene. It also facilitates the smooth flow of positive energy. Peace lilies look beautiful and are relatively low maintenance.

They do not require much light, so they can be placed in windowless rooms.

Orchids

Feng Shui experts believe that orchids act as lightning rods for positive energy, promoting great emotional and spiritual health. They are well known for their charming scent, which elevates the mood of all who smell it. To keep your orchid healthy, simply water it when the soil becomes dry.

Holy Basil

Used in Ayurvedic medicine as a means of cleansing the air of toxic energy, holy basil will give your home an instant energy boost. It can also be used to purify water, which can then be sprinkled in every room in your house to improve the flow of positive energy. To enjoy maximum benefit of this plant, place it in an east, north, or northeastern part of your house or garden.

OTHER WAYS TO CLEAR YOUR HOME OF NEGATIVE ENERGY

A messy home encourages negative energy to fester, whereas a clean, tidy space permits the flow of positive energy. Keep a clutter-free home when possible and get rid of objects you no longer use. This is particularly important if certain objects hold bad memories for you, as their negative energy can directly act on your body and mind. Repair broken objects, as they are another source of bad energy according to Feng Shui philosophy.

Make sure your home gets fresh air and sunlight. Draw back all the curtains and leave them open as long as possible. Open the windows for at least a few minutes every day. Fresh air purifies negative energy and helps you stay upbeat and optimistic.

Smudging is a quick and easy way to rid yourself and your home of negative energy. All you need to do is light a bundle of sage, blow it out, and then walk around your house whilst swirling the bundle in a counter-clockwise direction. Start in the hallway and work your way through every room.

Consider adding a water feature to your home. For instance, you could invest in a tabletop water fountain. The sound of running water is immensely soothing. Our bodies are primarily composed of water, and our water molecules are permanently in a state of vibration. If you raise the rate at which your water molecules vibrate, you can eliminate negative energy.

When you are close to an external source of water, its vibration will affect the water inside your body. The purer the external source, the more positive your internal energy will become. A moving water feature will therefore reduce the negative energy in your body, restoring a sense of tranquility and peace. If you do not like or cannot afford a moving water fountain, simply keeping a large transparent bowl of clean water in plain sight is an alternative option.

Finally, you can use saffron to eliminate negative energy from your surroundings. It emits a pungent scent that is said to repel negative energy and malevolent spirits. You can mix it in with water, leave it to steep for a few minutes, then sprinkle the infusion around your home to purify the environment.

PLAY BINAURAL BEATS & PURE TONES

Music changes the atmosphere of a home or workspace, and it can help clear negative energy fast. There are many free recordings of binaural beats and pure tones available online that will raise your body's vibration, stimulate your chakras, and help wash away a toxic aura. Some people find that listening to natural sounds, such as recordings of waves crashing against a shore, helps them restore their energy levels.

LAUGH

Laughter is one of the fastest ways to clear negative energy and make yourself feel better. When you've had a tough day, find something that makes you laugh, even if it's just a five-minute video on YouTube. Laughter triggers the release of endorphins in your brain, which lowers stress levels and can even act as natural painkillers.

Why not put together your own personal laughter library so you always have some funny material on hand whenever you need it? For instance, you could keep a shelf filled on your bookcase for light-hearted reads or compile a playlist of comedy recordings on your phone. If you like cartoons, keep a few stuck to your fridge or stick them on a pinboard near your desk.

CLAP & SING

The simple act of clapping your hands is enough to break up negative energy. Singing also promotes the flow of positive energy through your body and is a quick way to boost your mood. You might feel self-conscious at first, but after a couple of minutes, you'll be glad you tried it! For maximum effect, pair it with high-frequency music.

TRANSFORM YOUR NEGATIVE ENERGY INTO PRODUCTIVE ACTION

When a problem or person is dragging you down, challenge yourself to list at least three potential courses of action you can take to remedy the situation. For example, if you hate your job and arrive home each evening feeling burdened by negative energy, what could you come up with a plan of action that would either help you find a new position or at least enhance your current working environment?

If it's a person who keeps draining your energy, what could you do to improve your relationship with them? Sometimes it's as simple as making a few adjustments to your routine to minimize the amount of contact you have with them, such as choosing to take lunchtime a bit earlier or later to avoid running into a toxic colleague.

Let me be clear—not every situation is so easy to solve, and sometimes the best we can do is use tools that clear negative energy whilst making the most of a suboptimal job or relationship. However, many people get so caught up in their own negativity that it doesn't occur to them to sit down, carefully weigh their options, and channel their energy into devising a solution that will make them feel better. Empower yourself by taking a realistic look at your life and thinking about what you can personally do to change it.

OFFER OTHERS A HELPING HAND
When you help someone else, you spread positive energy and make the world a brighter place. Not only will the person you are helping feel grateful, but your self-esteem will also skyrocket. Showing someone else kindness is instant proof that you really can make a difference—you are here for a reason!

SPEND TIME WITH ANIMALS & PETS
Research has shown that people with pets tend to live longer, have stronger immune systems, enjoy better cardio-vascular health, and report lower levels of stress. Therapy animals are often brought into residential homes for elderly people and those with disabilities. There is no doubt that pets are a powerful source of healing.

Playing with a cat or dog will quickly improve your mood and help eliminate any negative energy you've accu-mulated throughout the day. Their life force ("chi") will raise your energy. Animals live in the present; they do not waste time worrying about the past or fearing the future. We have much to learn from them. Watching wild animals in a park or in the woods can also be relaxing.

PROTECTING YOURSELF FROM NEGATIVE ENERGY—SHIELDING

As the saying goes, prevention is better than cure. As an HSP, mastering the art of shielding yourself against negative energy will save you a lot of trouble. Shielding protects you from emotional contagion, meaning that you won't automatically pick up on everyone else's emotions. Just as a regular shield protects a soldier from enemy blows, an energy shield will deflect aggression, hopelessness, and other negative emotions that other people may knowingly or unintentionally send your way.

You can shield yourself in three simple steps.

1. Imagine a wall or barrier separating your body from everyone and everything around you. This barrier can take the form of a ring of light, a gate, or a glowing shield. Some people find it easier to imagine that they are wrapped in a white light. It doesn't matter what form your shield takes as long as it helps you feel safe.

2. Remind yourself that you can choose what passes through the shield. Picture yourself receiving good energy and positivity in the form of smiles, compliments, and sincere words of praise. Allow yourself to imagine feeling uplifting, secure, and content.

3. Visualize your shield keeping out bad energy. Imagine negative energy simply bouncing off it and away from everyone in the room. Remind

yourself that you get to choose what can and can't penetrate your barrier.

If you know in advance that you will be exposing yourself to negative energy—for example, if you are attending a meeting with tense, angry, or pessimistic people—meditate privately for a few minutes beforehand. Take this time to breathe deeply, ground yourself in the present, and engage in creative visualization.

Resist the urge to reflect someone's negative energy back in their direction. This is difficult to do because when someone else engages in negative behavior, it's tempting to give them a taste of their own medicine. For example, if someone makes a sarcastic remark, you may feel inclined to give a cutting answer. However, this approach helps nobody. At best, it maintains the negative energy in the environment. At worst, it culminates in open conflict that hurts both parties.

You have many options when it comes to eliminating negative energy from yourself and your surroundings. As an HSP, learning how to handle negative energy is a skill you must learn for the sake of your physical and emotional wellbeing. You don't need to remember every tip and technique—just experiment to find two or three that work for you and be ready to use them the moment you suspect your energy balance has been disturbed.

CHAPTER 6

Dealing with Depression as an HSP

High sensitivity isn't a mental illness, but some HSPs are at an increased risk of depression and anxiety compared with the general population. Fortunately, a few lifestyle adjustments, coupled with self-awareness, can safeguard your mental health. In the following chapters, you'll learn why some HSPs are more prone to mental illness than others, and what you can do if you notice the signs of depression or anxiety.

HSPs and Depression

Depression is a serious mental illness that affects around 20% of the population at some stage in their lives. Depression isn't simply a bad mood—its main symptoms include feelings of hopelessness, and lack of energy, weight changes, inappropriate guilt, and decreased motivation. If you think you might be depressed, it's important to make an appointment with your doctor.

Psychologists don't know for sure what causes depression, but most Western doctors believe that it is caused by an imbalance of chemicals within the brain. People with depression often experience symptoms following a stressful time in their lives, but it can also start for no apparent reason. This can also apply to HSPs. In other words, you don't need a reason to be depressed.

However, although each case is different, HSPs appear to be especially vulnerable in certain situations. Let's start by looking at the most common reasons HSPs become depressed.

Overstimulation, Helplessness, & Depression

When an HSP is chronically overstimulated, they may come to feel helpless, and helplessness can be a precursor to depression. Psychologists have long known that if someone feels as though they have no control over their own lives, they are prone to feelings of despair and depression. For example, suppose an HSP starts a new office job, and within a few days, they realize that the environment is far too noisy for them; in fact, they keep getting headaches and even feeling nauseated at the thought of going into work.

What could the HSP do in this situation? They could quit their job, but that probably isn't a good idea unless they have another lined up. Asking their boss and coworkers for reasonable accommodations, such as permission to work with headphones on when possible, would probably be a better idea.

However, let's say that their boss isn't particularly sympathetic and just tells the HSP to get on with their work. In this kind of situation, an HSP is forced to stay in an environment that causes them a lot of distress. Knowing that there is nothing they can do, they will likely become depressed. To make matters worse, the more depressed they feel, the less energy they will have to look for solutions such as finding alternative employment.

FEELING LOST OR "DIFFERENT" CAN TRIGGER DEPRESSION

Another reason an HSP may become depressed is that they don't understand why they feel so different from everyone around them. They may become lonely and come to the conclusion that they will never find someone who truly understands them. It can be hard to strike a balance between pursuing relationships on one hand and seeking solitude on the other. It can take years to find the right match, and the wait can take a toll on an HSP's morale.

JUDY DYER

Paying Attention to the State of the World Can Trigger Depression

An HSP can easily become despondent at the state of the world. There's no denying the sheer amount of suffering experienced by animals and humans alike. Even non-HSPs sometimes despair when they contemplate poverty, disease, and so forth. Over time, an HSP may feel almost grief-stricken by the thought that they can't do anything to fix the world's problems.

To make matters worse, they may wonder why those around them don't seem too concerned. They may come to believe that they "care too much" and that they need to "toughen up." Some HSPs have decided, whether consciously or not, that it's best to try to ignore the bad things that happen in the world. This might help them feel less distressed in the short term, but emotional suppression isn't healthy. In some cases, it can lead to an inability to feel any emotions at all, which increases a person's vulnerability to depression.

Perfectionism

HSPs tend to be deep thinkers, and they often hold themselves to high standards. On the plus side, this can make them very successful. However, there is a dark side to perfectionism. If you are a perfectionist, any mistake—even if it's relatively minor—will be a blow to your sense of identity. Of course, maintaining high standards over a long period of time is mentally and physically draining, which increases vulnerability to depression and burnout.

57

Depression & Burnout in HSPs

Burnout is a state of total depletion in which an individual experiences mental and physical exhaustion. Although it can result in a crisis (sometimes known as a "breakdown"), it's more likely to take the form of a slow decline. Someone in a state of burnout becomes numb to the world around them. They literally cannot take on new tasks and see no point in carrying on. In extreme cases, burned-out people require several months of rehabilitation before they recover fully.

Unfortunately, HSPs are more prone to burnout than non-HSPs. In the workplace, an HSP is usually forced to deal with busy environments, high workloads, office politics, and the pressure to conform. This is why many HSPs prefer to be self-employed—they get to manage their own environment and workload and can take a step back as soon as they identify the earliest signs of burnout.

Your Early Environment & Depression

For both HSPs and non-HSPs alike, being raised in an unhealthy environment can increase someone's vulnerability to depression in later life. For instance, we know that those who were abused as children are at significantly higher risk of mental illness as adults.

HSPs are especially susceptible to depression if they grew up in an unsupportive, invalidating environment. A sensitive child living in a dysfunctional household will be bombarded by other people's negative emotions, and this experience leaves long-lasting psychological wounds. On the other hand, an HSP who was accepted and loved as a child is somewhat protected against depression. However, they can still suffer if they are stuck in a seemingly hopeless situation or feel alienated from the rest of society.

DO YOU SPEND TIME WITH NEGATIVE OR DEPRESSED PEOPLE?

As an HSP, you feel both your own emotions and those of others keenly. On the plus side, this makes you a wonderful and supportive friend. Unfortunately, your tendency to absorb other people's feelings puts you at risk of emotional contagion. Whilst you can't "catch" depression, you can certainly feel low or even despondent if you spend too much time with someone you know or suspect to be depressed. It takes a strong HSP to maintain a healthy relationship with someone fighting depression, but you can help them while protecting yourself. Check in with yourself and set some firm boundaries.

For example, if you notice that someone has fallen into the habit of calling you several times a week in order to talk about their problems, you need to check in with yourself and take an inventory of how these interactions make you feel. If you realize that your conversations with this person leave you feeling down for several hours afterward, it's time to let them know that you need to either cut back on the number of conversations you have with them or talk about more positive (or just neutral) topics instead.

HOW TO HANDLE DEPRESSION AS AN HSP

As you can see, there are many reasons you might become depressed as an HSP. So, how can you safeguard your mental health? It depends on the reason you feel low, but here are some tips.

ACCEPT THAT YOU ARE DIFFERENT

Acknowledging your status as an HSP is helpful and healing. Thanks to the numerous online communities that have sprung up on the internet, you no longer have to feel alone. There are plenty of supportive blogs and websites that will help you make the most of your special trait. When you take a healthy pride in being an HSP and connect with others, you will no longer feel alienated. Given that 20% of the population is an HSP, you might also be able to find another HSP and support one another. Look out for those in your work or school that might be highly sensitive. Try to strike up a friendly conversation. You might make a new friend.

GET ENOUGH TIME ALONE

We've already established that HSPs require a lot of space. If you lead a busy lifestyle, it's easy to fill your schedule up to the extent that you don't have time for yourself. All too often, HSPs suddenly realize that their lives are too full and they have little opportunity to retreat from the outside world.

Schedule time for yourself in the same way you would plan any activity, and honor that commitment. Yes, your work and relationships are important, but spending time alone is essential for your mental health. Think in advance of what you would like to do during these periods. Just sitting in a relaxing bath with a good book might be all you need to feel better after a tough day.

Work on Leading a Healthier Lifestyle

Most of us know that our bodies and minds are interlinked. The saying "Healthy mind, healthy body" is a cliché for a reason. Cutting down on alcohol, reducing your intake of processed foods, getting more exercise, sticking to a regular sleep schedule, and making time to relax for at least a few minutes every day can do wonders for your mental health.

Focus on Forming & Maintaining Positive Relationships

If spending time with depressing people is hurting your mental health, what's the antidote? Spending time with uplifting people, of course! You are readily influenced by other people's moods, so use it to your advantage. Even if you are highly introverted, try to socialize with those who lift you up at least a couple of times each month. When you have no choice but to interact with negative people, use your shielding skills to protect yourself from emotional harm.

Learn How to Challenge Negative Thoughts

Depression is a complex illness with many possible causes and manifestations, but most professionals believe that it is sustained by habitual negative thinking. For example, many depressed people assume that they are boring, unappealing, and have little to offer the world. They may regularly think to themselves, "No one would ever want to talk to me," "I'm utterly useless," or "I'm not worth listening to."

You can see how this type of negative thinking keeps depression going. It's like having a bully following you around all day, whispering (or shouting) nasty things in your ear. Even the most naturally optimistic person would struggle to feel happy if they had to listen to unrelenting negativity all day.

Fortunately, you can learn to identify and challenge your negative thoughts. This exercise will help you.

1. Identify your negative thought and write it down.

2. Note how the thought makes you feel. For example, if you think, "I am ugly," you may feel worthless or upset as a result.

3. Ask yourself the following questions, and think carefully about the answers.

   • Do I have any evidence that contradicts the negative thought?

   • What would I say to someone else in the same situation?

   • Is this a helpful way to think?

   • Can I think of a more balanced thought that won't make me feel as bad?

This process won't be easy at first but with enough practice, you'll be able to do it anywhere. It doesn't matter whether you actually believe your new balanced thoughts at first—a depressed brain requires serious retraining. You may wish to check out books on Cognitive Behavioral Therapy (CBT) to learn more techniques to challenge your negative thoughts. If you feel overwhelmed by the prospect of doing this work alone, consider seeing a therapist.

CONSULT A THERAPIST OR COACH WHO CAN HELP YOU MAKE CHANGES IN YOUR LIFE

As you know, feelings of helplessness can result in depression. To tackle the root cause, you need to identify the areas of your life that need fixing and devise a plan of action that will help you take back control. Learning how to handle your emotions will help you deal with emotional overwhelm and depression in the short term but the only viable long-term solution is to take a long, hard look at your lifestyle and situation and make whatever adjustments are necessary for your mental health.

Unfortunately, it can be hard to do this alone, particularly if your motivation has disappeared and you aren't even sure how to begin fixing your problems. This is where a good therapist or coach can help you. They can provide an objective view of your situation, equip you with the skills you need to solve your own problems, and provide emotional support as you make changes. They can also help you work through maladaptive thought patterns and take a more positive approach to life.

You can ask a medical practitioner to refer you to a psychotherapist or you can search for a qualified professional by visiting the official websites of counseling training and regulatory bodies. For example, in the US, you can find a therapist at counselling.org, the website of the American Counseling Association.

Earlier in this chapter, you learned that some HSPs may be prone to depression if they grew up in a disturbed or chaotic home. If this applies to you, you might also need to process difficult childhood experiences and work through past trauma with the help of your therapist.

Don't Forget to Cleanse Yourself of Negative Energy

In Chapter 5, we looked at how and why you should be proactive in eliminating negative energy from your home and life. When you sense that your mood is about to take a downward turn, consciously choose to eliminate negative energy from your body and space. Set aside an afternoon to clean and tidy your home. Ask a friend or relative for help if you are low on energy and motivation.

When you are depressed, basic self-care can be a chore. Grounding, smudging, meditation, and other helpful techniques that you would usually enjoy can feel impossible. Do not push yourself too hard. Challenge yourself to do one thing every day that helps remove toxic energy from your life. For instance, you could try 10 minutes of meditation practice one day and promise yourself to cleanse your home of negative energy by smudging it the next.

CONSIDER COMPLEMENTARY TREATMENT OPTIONS

If you feel depressed, it's important to see your regular doctor. They can carry out tests to ensure that your symptoms are not caused by another condition, such as thyroid problems. If you receive a diagnosis of depression, you might be advised to take antidepressants.

Medication works for some people, but some HSPs find conventional treatments unpleasant and ineffective. Although antidepressants can cause side effects in anyone regardless of their sensitivity levels, HSPs are particularly vulnerable to nausea, skin rashes, digestive complaints, and other problems that can arise when taking these drugs. Of course, they are sometimes necessary to help an HSP through a crisis. If you have been prescribed a drug, you should never stop taking it without consulting a medical professional.

Complementary therapies that involve energy work can also be useful for HSPs who struggle with depression. For example, you could consider seeking out a Reiki practitioner. Reiki is a form of energy healing based on the theory that a trained therapist can facilitate the movement of energy from their hands to a patient's body merely by using the power of touch. According to Reiki practitioners, we all have "life force energy" that powers our bodies and minds. If these energy levels drop, the result is fatigue and susceptibility to illness. During a Reiki session, a therapist restores the body's life force energy, which leads to feelings of relaxation, positivity, and peace. You remain fully clothed throughout the treatment, and there is no pain or discomfort involved.

YOU CAN DO IT!

Depression is a frightening illness, but you don't have to suffer alone. Although there is still a stigma surrounding mental illness, people are more willing to talk about these issues than ever before. Being an HSP does not mean you are doomed to live a life ruled by your emotions, and neither does it mean that you are destined to get depression. In fact, if you take charge of your self-development and learn how to work with your feelings, you will actually be safeguarding yourself against mental illness.

CHAPTER 7

Dealing with Anxiety as an HSP

An HSP who lacks insight into their special trait might assume that they are just a jittery, anxious person destined to live a life of worry. Fortunately, it doesn't have to be this way. As you've made your way through this book, you will have come to appreciate why an HSP can easily feel overwhelmed and anxious. In fact, it's almost inevitable—being caught in a tsunami of emotions and energy fields naturally has a significant impact on a person's wellbeing. The good news is that when you develop self-awareness and self-management skills, you won't have to suffer from chronic anxiety.

THE DIFFERENCE BETWEEN HIGH SENSITIVITY & ANXIETY

To the untrained eye, high sensitivity and anxiety disorders appear similar. In fact, many people use the words "sensitive" and "anxious" interchangeably. For example, someone with a phobia of small spaces will have panic attacks whenever they have to spend time in a large crowd. Their symptoms—feeling overwhelmed, shaky, jittery, and physically unwell—are the same as those reported by HSPs when they are highly stimulated.

Although not all people with anxiety disorders are HSPs and not all HSPs have anxiety disorders, there is a link between anxiety and sensitivity. HSPs tend to have particularly sensitive startle reflexes, which make them more prone to heightened emotional arousal. An individual's reflexes are determined by their genetics, which partially explains why HSPs typically report that sensitivity seems to run in their family.

Just to make matters worse, the average HSP has a vivid imagination that can fuel their anxieties even further. This is a downside of creativity! They are all too capable of imagining worst-case scenarios, which further feeds into their anxiety or panic. For example, if they feel especially shaken in a noisy environment, they may start to wonder whether they are having a heart attack and even begin to worry how their family or friends will deal with the news of their death! This may sound melodramatic or ridiculous to a non-HSP, but the distress people with this trait feel is real.

The key difference, of course, is that non-HSPs with

anxiety disorders can approach their anxiety as a mental illness that can be eliminated entirely with the right treatment. On the other hand, an HSP will never fully eliminate their sensitivity and susceptibility to anxiety and panic. If you are a particularly anxious HSP, aim to get your tendency to worry under control rather than to overcome it completely. You can help yourself cope with high levels of intense stimuli, but you will always have a lower stress threshold than a non-HSP.

Tips for Anxious HSPs

Ride the Wave of Anxiety – Don't Try to Fight It
The best way to combat anxious thoughts and panic attacks is to accept what is happening and ride them out. Resisting your feelings will only make them worse. Think of it like this—if someone tells you not to think about a polar bear, what happens? You think about a polar bear, of course! The same principle applies here.

It's impossible to shut down a panic attack once your nervous system has sprung into action. When you begin to panic, your body releases adrenalin that triggers your fight-or-flight response. At this point, you have a choice to either try to reason your body out of its symptoms or choose to accept what is happening and wait it out.

Therapist Linda Walter, who specializes in working with anxious people, recommends the R.I.D.E. technique. It's a simple acronym that can help you handle even the roughest of panic attacks!

Recognize: Acknowledge that you are having a panic attack.

Involve: Choose to engage with your surroundings. Use grounding and breathing exercises to keep yourself rooted in the present.

Distract: This step is self-explanatory. All you need to do is find something that holds your attention, even if it's just for a few moments.

End: Trust that even the scariest of panic attacks usually pass within a few minutes, and almost all attacks end within 30 minutes.

It may not feel like it, but anxiety can't kill you. You have the strength to make it through to the other side!

A mantra is another useful tool. Come up with a phrase or saying in advance and repeat it to yourself during difficult times. For instance, you could tell yourself, "This will pass," or "I just need to wait." Write it on a card and keep it in your purse or wallet so you have it on hand. You could even make it your phone wallpaper!

Master Breathing Exercises

Breathing exercises can make you feel better during times of high anxiety. Practice slow, deep breathing when you are calm until it becomes second nature. You will then be able to use this technique when anxiety strikes. To calm yourself down, begin by inhaling through your nose. Picture the air filling your lungs. Hold your breath whilst counting to three. Purse your lips and exhale slowly. As you breathe out, make a conscious effort to relax your body. Pay particular attention to your neck, shoulders, stomach, and jaw.

A variation of this exercise is the "Calming Counts" technique. Find a comfortable place if possible and sit down. Begin by inhaling slowly and deeply. As you exhale, tell yourself to relax. Next, take ten normal breaths. Shut your eyes and keep them closed as you count down, either in your head or out loud. You can also ask someone else to count for you if you feel very worried and unable to concentrate. As you do this exercise, make a conscious effort to relax the muscles in your body.

Watch for Patterns

Some people find that their feelings of worry and panic appear to come and go at random, but there are usually some underlying triggers. Pay close attention to the events preceding your periods of anxiety and panic. You can then make a plan of action. For example, if you seem to get anxious around a particular person, you will need to work on your energy shielding, use your boundary-setting skills, or learn how to resolve disagreements. If a particular environment makes you feel tense and panicky, use the techniques outlined in this book to cleanse it of negative energy.

Remember that if you are generally stressed and anxious, it won't take much to tip you over the edge into a panic attack or a state of emotional overwhelm. To thrive as an HSP, you will benefit from getting into healthy habits that will help you manage stress, such as regular meditation and energy work.

Finding a Sympathetic Mental Health Professional

If your feelings of anxiety are causing you a lot of distress, or you are having problems functioning at home or work, you should consider seeking professional help. However, it's important that you choose a doctor or therapist who appreciates that some people are simply more sensitive than others, and therefore have different needs. You may need to take anti-anxiety medication if your symptoms are severe, but it's usually more effective to take a long-term approach and learn to manage your own feelings.

For example, a non-HSP who has developed an anxiety disorder following a difficult period in their life can reasonably expect to make a full recovery and return to their usual low levels of anxiety, but an HSP should not be encouraged to change their personality just to fit in with society's idea of "normal."

When attending an initial consultation, ask whether they are accustomed to working with HSPs. If they aren't familiar with the term, say something like, "You see a lot of people, so you know that some people are just naturally more sensitive. I'm in that camp!" You could even bring some literature on high sensitivity with you. A caring, open-minded health professional should be willing to listen. If not, find someone else who is more on your wavelength.

UNDERSTANDING YOUR PAST

In the same way that past experiences can lay the foundations for depression, they can also make you more prone to worry and anxiety. For example, if you were bullied as a child or teenager, you might be reluctant to trust others and find yourself panicking in social situations. Sometimes, simply becoming aware of these patterns is enough to help you feel better. However, working with a therapist is beneficial if your worries are deep-seated.

MAKE CHANGES TO YOUR DIET

No one eats a perfectly healthy diet all the time, but it's worth making a few changes because your diet can make a huge difference in how you feel. Don't aim for perfection, because you'll only make yourself more anxious!

Cut Down on Sugar

Too much sugar can lead to difficulty concentrating, visual disturbances, and fatigue. Sugar highs lead to dramatic crashes, which can come with the physical and psychological symptoms associated with anxiety such as shaking and feelings of panic. Although sugar does not directly cause panic attacks, its effects can make you feel as though you might have one, and your worries can bring on the real thing.

Skip the Fruit Juice

Do you prefer to drink juice rather than eat whole fruit? If so, it might be time to cut back. When you eat a piece of fruit, your body digests it slowly. The sugar hits your blood-stream at a modest rate. However, when you drink juice, your blood sugar will suddenly spike before crashing soon after, which can worsen or trigger anxiety.

Pass On the Alcohol

Alcohol can help you feel calm, but the effects are only temporary. You risk developing an alcohol dependency if you get into the habit of using it to help you relax. You will also disrupt your blood sugar and sleep schedule after just a couple of glasses, which won't help you feel better!

Reduce Your Caffeine Intake

Be careful not to drink too much caffeine. Stick to one or two caffeinated drinks per day and avoid it after 2 p.m. You may find that even a little bit of caffeine is too much and choose to cut it out of your diet altogether. Remember, HSPs often have sensitive bodies that react strongly to stimulants. Chocolate contains caffeine (along with processed sugar), so restrict your intake to a small amount of once or twice a week.

Experiment with a Gluten-Free Diet

Many people with gluten intolerance and celiac disease report feelings of anxiety. Research carried out with celiac patients suggests that their anxiety levels drop once they have cut out gluten for a year, and some doctors believe that people with non-celiac gluten sensitivity are also prone to feelings of anxiety when they ingest gluten. Dr. Rodney

Ford, who has a special interest in the effects of gluten on the body, believes that it might trigger or overstimulate the nervous system, giving rise to feelings of worry and panic. Given that HSPs have highly reactive nervous systems, it makes sense that they might be more sensitive to gluten than the average individual.

There is relatively little work in this area to date, but anecdotal evidence suggests that eliminating gluten may be effective in controlling anxiety in some individuals. If your anxiety hasn't responded to self-help, therapy, or medication, you could try a gluten-free diet. However, it's best to work with a doctor or dietitian if you want to try this kind of eating plan as it can result in malnutrition if not carried out under proper supervision.

CARRY CRYSTALS

Blue lace agate, rose quartz, and black tourmaline are just three crystals commonly recommended by healers treating people with anxiety. They carry positive vibrational energy that has a soothing effect on the nervous system. To get the most benefit from a crystal, wear it as a piece of jewelry so that it is in constant contact with your skin. If this isn't possible, you can carry a crystal in your pocket. When you meditate, hold a crystal in the palm of your hand to cleanse yourself of stress and tension.

When choosing a crystal, allow your intuition to guide you. If you feel that a particular stone is right for you, that's the one you should buy! To cleanse them of negative energy, leave them in strong sunlight or moonlight for a few hours.

Anxiety is a common problem for HSPs. Fortunately, there are many steps you can take to help regulate your mood and control your worries. The best approach is to combine a healthy lifestyle with self-awareness, energy work, and specific techniques you can use to help you deal with panic attacks and waves of anxiety.

CONCLUSION

Congratulations on taking the first step forward on your journey as an HSP! When you picked up this book, you probably felt somewhat nervous or perhaps even skeptical. That's completely normal—not many HSPs know that their personality type has a name and that there are millions of others out there who share their experiences.

Now that you understand what it really means to be an HSP, you will see yourself and your past in a new light. This paves the way to self-acceptance, which is one of the most precious gifts of all. No longer will you wonder why some people and places have such a dramatic effect on you, and no longer will you feel helpless in the face of your own emotions.

Remember that personal growth is a lifelong endeavor. Go at your own pace. For example, you may wish to focus on learning to cleanse yourself of negative energy first before reevaluating your relationships. Just like any other skill, self-mastery becomes easier over time.

May your journey be fulfilling and joyous!

THANKS FOR READING!

I hope this book has helped you come to terms with your needs as an HSP and that you have enjoyed reading it as much as I enjoyed writing it!

It would mean a lot to me if you left an Amazon review—I will reply to all questions!

https://www.amazon.com/review/create-review?asin=B07GY3BF6C

Be sure to check out my email list, where I am constantly adding tons of value.

The best way to currently get on it is by visiting http://pristinepublish.com/forgive and entering your email.

Here I'll provide actionable information that aims to improve your enjoyment of life.

I'll update you on my latest books and I'll even send free e-books that I think you'll find useful.

Kindest regards,

Judy Dyer

Also by
Judy Dyer

Grasp a better understanding of your gift and how you can embrace every part of it so that your life is enriched day by day.

Visit: amazon.com/Judy-Dyer/e/B077P7TG99

SOURCES

American Psychiatric Association. (2013). *DSM-V.* Retrieved from autismspectrum.org.au

Anderson, J. (2018). *Is Anxiety a Common Symptom in Gluten Disorders?* verywellmind.com

Anxieties.com. (n.d.) *STEP 4: Practice Your Breathing Skills.* anxieties.com

Aron, E. (2013). *How Do You Recognize an HSP?* hsperson.com

Aron, E. (2018). *FAQ.* hsperson.com

Aron, E. (n.d.). *FAQ.* hsperson.com

Brandt, A. (2015). *What to Do When Your Emotions Overwhelm You.* psychologytoday.com

Clusters of Inspiration. (2016). *EQ meets HSP: Emotional Intelligence and the Highly Sensitive Person.* clustersofinspiration.com

Newman, S. (2016). How Highly Sensitive People Can Shield Themselves From Negativity. psychcentral.com

O'Laughlan, K. (n.d.) HSPs and Depression. highlysensitiveperson.net

Orloff, J. (2017). The Differences Between Highly Sensitive People and Empaths. psychologytoday.com

Psychology Today. (n.d.) *Emotional Intelligence.* psychologytoday.com

Smit, A.W. (n.d.) *10 must-know misconceptions about (high) sensitive people.* ankewebersmit.com

Top10HomeRemedies. (n.d.) *How to Remove Negative Energy from Your Home.* top10homeremedies.com

Top10HomeRemedies. (2016). *10 Plants that Attract Positive Energy.* top10homeremedies.com

Walter, L. (2011). *R.I.D.E. the Wave of Panic.* psychologytoday.com

Ward, D. (2012). *Coping with Anxiety as an HSP.* psychologytoday.com

Made in the USA
Monee, IL
06 July 2020

35950570R00056